# The Sky Painter

## LOUIS FUERTES, BIRD ARTIST

**two lions**

*For Curtis, my lifelong bird-watching partner, with lifelong love –M.E.*

*These illustrations are for all those who admire and love the beauty of soaring birds in the sky. –A.B.*

ACKNOWLEDGMENTS

I thank God for birds and for the people who protect their habitats.

I am indebted to the archives of Cornell University, the expedition diaries of Frank M. Chapman, *To a Young Bird Artist* by Louis Fuertes (Univ. of Oklahoma Press, 1979), *Louis Agassiz Fuertes* by Mary Boynton Fuertes (Oxford Univ. Press, 1956), and *A Celebration of Birds* by Robert McCracken Peck (Walker, 1982).

For encouragement, I am grateful to my family, Carmen T. Bernier-Grand, Sandra Ríos Balderrama, Alma Flor Ada, and Isabel Campoy.

Special thanks to my agent, Michelle Humphrey; illustrator Aliona Bereghici; and my editor, Robin Benjamin (and her helper, Everett), Katrina Damkoehler, Kelsey Skea, and the entire publishing team.

–M.E.

Images on page 40: "Fuertes with Snowy Owl" photograph, source: Louis Agassiz Fuertes Papers, #2662. Division of Rare and Manuscript Collections, Cornell University Library; "Mallard Duck" painting by Louis A. Fuertes, source: Division of Rare and Manuscript Collections, Cornell University Library; "Woodpeckers" painting by Louis A. Fuertes, courtesy of Cornell Lab of Ornithology, birds.cornell.edu.

Special thanks to Kevin McGowan, Ph.D., for his guidance on the portrayal of the birds in this book.

Published by Two Lions, New York
www.apub.com
Amazon, the Amazon logo, and Two Lions are trademarks of Amazon.com, Inc., or its affiliates
ISBN-13: 9781477826331 (Hardcover)  ISBN-10: 1477826335 (Hardcover)
ISBN-13: 9781477876329 (eBook)  ISBN-10: 1477876324 (eBook)

The illustrations were rendered in watercolor and ink.
Book design by Ryan Michaels
Printed in China (R)
FIRST EDITION
10 9 8 7 6 5 4 3 2 1

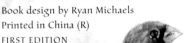

# The Sky Painter

## LOUIS FUERTES, BIRD ARTIST

*by*
**Margarita Engle**

*illustrated by*
**Aliona Bereghici**

# Helping Birds

I love the bright wings of birds
as they fly, wild and free,
high above me.

When I watch birds in flight,
I dream of soaring too!

Indigo Bunting
male

Indigo Bunting
female

I care for injured birds
in my little hospital
under our front porch.

Papi scolds in Spanish,
and Mama scolds in English;
but I think a messy porch is fine.

I love helping weak birds
grow strong enough to return
to the sky.

# Bird Art

I carry an orphaned owl
into the kitchen.

Gently, I tie his leg
to the leg
of the table.

The owl poses calmly, looking so wise
that I imagine he must know
all sorts of owl secrets.

When I sketch his round eyes,
the narrow pencil in my hand
feels as wide and free
as a wing
in wild sky.

Eastern Screech
Owl chick

# The Library

Papi wants me to be an engineer like him,
and Mama says I should listen to Papi;
but I dream of becoming a bird artist.

When Papi takes me to the library,
I find a huge book of bird art.

The book is so heavy
that a nice librarian
has to help me turn
the giant pages.

I feel as if I've entered
a magical world
of wings.

# Learning

When I am fourteen, I finally
have the chance to paint my first
brightly colored bird,
a red crossbill
with a funny beak.

I use a pen to sketch the outline
and watercolors to fill in the feathers.
Then I try adding more details
with ink, but my painting
starts to look muddy.

If I want to be a bird artist,
I can't get discouraged.
I need to practice.
I have to draw, draw, draw!

crossbills

L. Fuerte

Great
Crested
Flycatcher

American
Robin

Prothonotary
Warbler

Belted Kingfisher

White-breasted
Nuthatch

Eastern
Screech
Owl

Eastern
Bluebird

Dark-eyed
Junco

New

# Birds, Birds, Birds!

At school I listen to birdsongs
while I sit in the classroom
beside an open window.

At home I paint, and when my family
travels to Europe, I practice painting
birds in Paris, birds in Switzerland,
rare birds, common birds,
beautiful birds,
funny birds. . . .

Cerulean Warbler

Red Crossbill

Mourning Dove

American Crow

American Goldfinch

Birds

When I'm finally old enough
to start college, I sketch my professors
as cartoon birds.

Papi scolds in Spanish, and Mama scolds
in English; but they are both proud
of my serious
bird art.

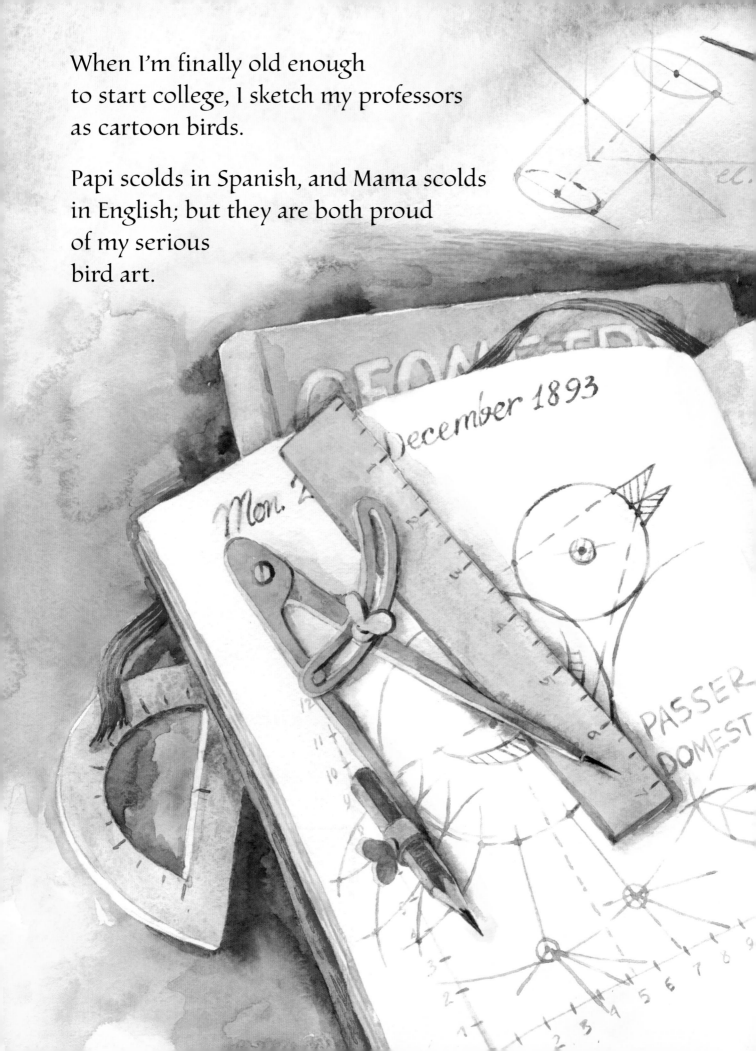

# Letting Birds Live

Bird artists are expected
to hunt with guns or slingshots,
then pose the dead skins,
arranging them in positions
that make them look
like living birds.

I learn to hunt, but I would rather
help birds survive, so I practice
painting quickly, while wings
swoop
and race
across
wild
blue
sky,
so swift,
and so alive!

Barn Swallow
female

Barn Swallow
male

# Understanding Birds

To learn about ducks,
I don't need to shoot them.

Mallard Duck
male

Mallard Duck
female

I plunge into a lake and look up
from below, studying their funny tails
and their paddling
webbed feet.

My paintings of birds in the sky,
and birds underwater, are accepted
by museums and printed in books.

Soon, I am invited to paint
in distant places, on expeditions
with scientists who explore
mountains, deserts, and jungles–
all the amazing natural habitats
where birds nest
and fly.

Florida
Wild Turkey
female

Florida Scrub-Jay

Florida
Wild Turkey
male

# Alaska

I whistle.
Birds answer.
I follow.
Blue shadows.
White snow.
Clear ice.
The beauty
of flight
like a dance
in the clouds,
a graceful ballet
of wild swans.

American Flamingo

# The Caribbean

On a small island near Puerto Rico,
where my father was born,

I sit on a beach and cover myself
with an invisibility cloak
of green palm leaves

so that I can hide quietly
and birds will come close,

unafraid of my brush
and the way my hand flies

as I rush to paint
brilliant pink flamingos
against a sunset sky.

# South America

In a boat on a misty river
in the cloud forest, I sing
in Spanish, while above me,
blue-and-gold macaws,
scarlet macaws,
green parrots,
and rainbow toucans
all sing along with their own
click, clack
tropical rhythms.

Howler monkeys join in,
whooping and roaring, while
my bird friends and I chuckle,
peep, croak, whistle, and shriek,
making our wild voices
rise up and soar!

Channel-billed
Toucan

Blue-and-Yellow
Macaw

Yellow-eared Parrot

Scarlet Macaw

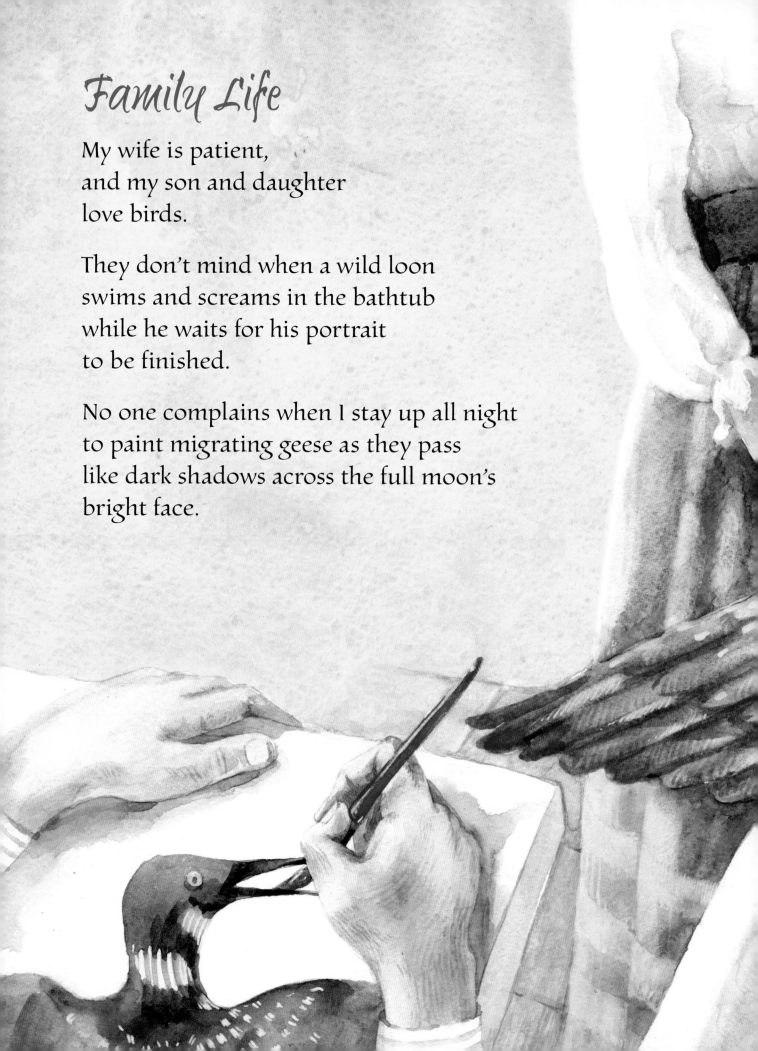

# Family Life

My wife is patient,
and my son and daughter
love birds.

They don't mind when a wild loon
swims and screams in the bathtub
while he waits for his portrait
to be finished.

No one complains when I stay up all night
to paint migrating geese as they pass
like dark shadows across the full moon's
bright face.

# The Natural-History Museum

Between expeditions I paint
huge murals of natural habitats
on museum walls.

Even though I'm shy,
I enjoy talking to children
who come to see my indoor sky.

When I see women wearing feathers
on their fancy hats, I politely suggest
other decorations–roses or ribbons–
so that rare birds
can survive.

# Africa

The thrill of another expedition!
I paint an enormous, brilliant-blue
silvery-cheeked hornbill.

I play with a baby baboon,
lion cubs, and cheetahs.

I love to experiment, so one day,
instead of painting birds, I sculpt
a statue of a mountain gorilla
with a delicate butterfly
perched
on his thumb.

Maybe people who see my statue
will understand that wild creatures
can be gentle.

# The Studio

Neighborhood children call me
the Bird Man.

When they peek into my studio,
I tell silly stories, squawk like a parrot,
and howl like a monkey.

Then I invite the children
to sketch their own funny
wild
silly
strange
beautiful
birds.

# Bird-watching

My bird paintings are printed
on cards that children
love to collect.

When I walk around the park,
I see people watching the sky
as they identify songbirds,
eagles, and egrets. . . .

All over the world, millions of people
have learned to enjoy, protect,
and celebrate
the wild beauty
of wings!

*If the birds of the world had met to select a human being who could best express to mankind the beauty and charm of their forms, their songs, their rhythmic flight, their manners for the heart's delight, they would unquestionably have chosen Louis Fuertes.* —FRANK M. CHAPMAN, ORNITHOLOGIST

## HISTORICAL NOTE

*Louis Agassiz Fuertes* was born in Ithaca, New York, in 1874. He was the youngest in a family of six children born to Mary Perry and Estévan Fuertes, a Puerto Rican engineering professor at Cornell University. Fuertes is known as the Father of Modern Bird Art, because he pioneered the painting of living birds in natural habitats. As a young boy, he was inspired by an elephant folio of John James Audubon's art. Later, Fuertes began his career as a bird artist in the traditional way, hunting so that he could pose dead birds as models. When

he decided that he wanted to let the birds live, Fuertes realized that he would face a challenge. Birds move swiftly, so he had to learn to paint quickly. As his skills developed, he was able to show birds in action. His paintings showed life in the birds' eyes and motion in their wings. He had created an entirely new form of bird art.

Fuertes illustrated most of the great bird books of his era and painted the habitat murals at the American Museum of Natural History in New York. When he wasn't away on expeditions, he lived in Ithaca with his wife and two children, and taught at Cornell University, where his letters are archived. Many of his paintings are in the Academy of Natural Sciences in Philadelphia.

Roger Tory Peterson and other ornithologists have described Fuertes as the greatest bird artist who ever lived. Beginning in the 1920s, collectors' cards of Fuertes's paintings were included in boxes of Arm & Hammer Baking Soda. The cards turned bird-watching into America's most popular sport and helped make wildlife conservation a way of life.